A COLD IS NOTHING TO SNEEZE AT

Designed by Bill Foster of Albarella & Associates, Inc.

Distributed to schools and libraries
in the United States by
ENCYCLOPAEDIA BRITANNICA EDUCATIONAL CORP.
310 South Michigan Ave.
Chicago, Illinois 60604

Library of Congress Cataloging-in-Publication Data

Perry, Susan, 1950-
Nothing to sneeze at/by Susan Perry; Anastasia Mitchell,
illustrator.
p. cm.
Summary: Discusses the causes and effects of the
common cold and ways to deal with it.
ISBN 0-89565-819-4
1. Cold (Disease) — Juvenile literature. [1. Cold
(Disease)]
I. Mitchell, Anastasia, ill.   II. Title
RF361.P47   1992
616.2'05 — dc20   91-29452
                                                        CIP
                                                        AC

A COLD IS NOTHING TO SNEEZE AT

Written by Susan Perry

Illustrated by Anastasia Mitchell

THE CHILD'S WORLD

You're sitting there, minding your own business, when… **ZAP!**…a cold invades your body. For a couple of days, you don't feel a thing. Then your throat gets a bit sore, or your nose starts running, or you begin to sneeze and cough. Maybe all these things happen at once.

If you're like most kids, colds invade your body about three times a year. Having a cold is not as bad as having the flu or chicken pox, but it can still make you feel pretty lousy for two or three days. And sometimes a cold can lead to a more serious illness, like pneumonia.

Colds can also keep you from doing things that you like to do. Have you ever missed an important event because you had a cold? Like a birthday party? A championship soccer game? Or a family picnic? Or maybe you've had to stay home from school because of a cold. Each year some 60 million days of school are missed by kids with colds.

In 1969, three Apollo 9 astronauts caught colds and had to delay their trip into space for one week. The delay cost half a million dollars!

AH-CHOO!

So you see, a cold is nothing to sneeze at.

A COLD QUIZ

People get colds more often than any other illness. Yet most people don't understand colds. They believe things about colds that aren't really true.

How about you? How much of what you know about colds is fact and how much is fiction? Listed below are some common beliefs about colds. Are they true or false?

If you go outside in winter with wet hair, you'll catch a cold.

☐ **True** ☐ **False**

Drinking from a glass that belongs to someone who has a cold is a sure way to catch a cold.

☐ **True** ☐ **False**

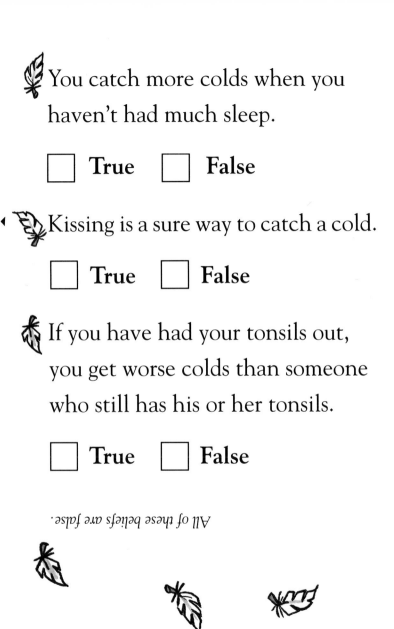

You catch more colds when you haven't had much sleep.

☐ **True** ☐ **False**

Kissing is a sure way to catch a cold.

☐ **True** ☐ **False**

If you have had your tonsils out, you get worse colds than someone who still has his or her tonsils.

☐ **True** ☐ **False**

All of these beliefs are false.

How well did you score? Now read on for the cold truth about colds.

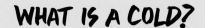

WHAT IS A COLD?

A cold is not one disease that you get over and over again. It's really as many as 200 different diseases. You can catch each of these cold diseases only once in a lifetime. Of course, there are so many of them that you could live to be 100 and still not catch them all.

WHO GETS COLDS?

Everyone gets colds from time to time, but some people get them more often than others. Have you ever noticed, for example, that you seem to get more colds than your parents?

Take an informal survey of some of the people you know. Ask each person how many colds he or she had during the last year. Try to include people of all different ages.

Now see if the results of your survey match what scientists have found out about colds:

❋ Kids get more colds than adults.

❋ Babies get more colds than anyone – about six before they are a year old.

❋ Until they are three years old, boys get more colds than girls.

❋ After the age of three, girls get more colds than boys.

❋ Adult women also get more colds than adult men. No one knows why for sure.

❋ People over the age of forty get fewer colds than younger people.

Getting colds seems to depend on your age and whether you're boy or a girl. The older you are, the fewer colds you get. And boys seem to get fewer colds than girls.

Where you live doesn't make much difference. People who live in warm climates get just as many colds as people who live in cold, damp climates.

WHERE DO COLDS COME FROM?

Colds are caused by collections of chemicals known as *viruses*. You need a special microscope to see viruses for they are very, very tiny. If you put ten million viruses in a line, the line would only be an inch long!

When seen through a microscope, viruses look like pretty snowflakes. But don't let that fool you. Viruses are mean stuff. Besides causing colds, they also cause diseases like polio, flu, measles, mumps, rabies, and even warts.

Viruses cause disease by invading and taking over cells in the body. But they are very fussy. Each virus likes to invade only one type of cell. The rabies virus, for example, only invades brain cells. The virus that causes warts only invades skin cells.

Cold viruses – all 200 or so of them – only invade cells in your nose and throat. But that's plenty of room to stir up a lot of trouble.

THE INVASION OF THE COLD VIRUS

Once a cold virus has invaded a cell, that cell is doomed to die. But as it's dying, it does something to save the cells around it. It releases a chemical called *interferon*. Interferon acts sort of like Paul Revere. It tells all the neighboring cells that a virus is coming and that they had better get ready for the attack. That helps slow down the invasion.

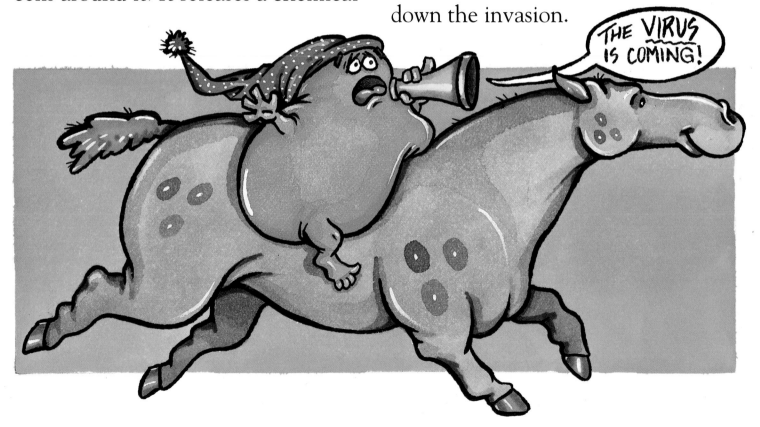

THE VIRUS IS COMING!

It also gives white blood cells time to come charging to the rescue. White blood cells live in your blood. When a cold invades, they leave the blood and go to your throat and nose where they kill and eat the viruses. The battle is fierce and it can go on for several days. Luckily, the good guys – the white blood cells – always win.

After the battle, the white blood cells leave behind a special group of guards, called *antibodies*. The antibodies patrol the bloodstream and make sure that the defeated cold virus never attacks again.

And that's why you can never get the same cold twice.

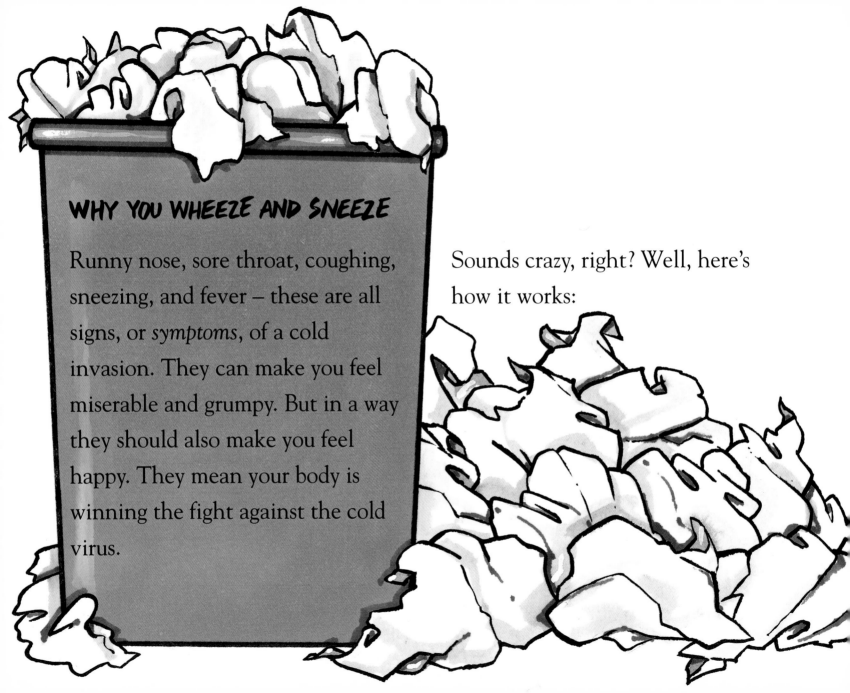

WHY YOU WHEEZE AND SNEEZE

Runny nose, sore throat, coughing, sneezing, and fever – these are all signs, or *symptoms*, of a cold invasion. They can make you feel miserable and grumpy. But in a way they should also make you feel happy. They mean your body is winning the fight against the cold virus.

Sounds crazy, right? Well, here's how it works:

For the white blood cells to come charging to the rescue, your body has to send extra blood to the cold's battle site – your nose and throat. The extra blood makes the inside of your nose and throat swell and turn red. That's why you get a sore throat.

That's also why you get a runny nose. When you are feeling well, the *mucus*, or sticky fluid that lines and protects the inside of your nose, usually creeps backwards toward your throat. Then it slides into your stomach, where it is destroyed. But when you have a cold, your nose gets too swollen for the mucus to move backwards. So it drips out of the front of your nose.

Sneezes help clear mucus from your stuffed-up nose – and from your mouth. Coughs do an even more important job. They keep mucus from getting into your lungs. Cold viruses like to hang out in mucus. If virus-infected mucus were to sneak into your lungs, you could get pneumonia. And that could be serious.

Some people – especially kids – get fevers with their colds. A fever happens when the temperature of your body goes higher than usual. No one knows what causes fevers, but some scientists think fevers help white blood cells come charging to the rescue.

HOW A COLD IS CAUGHT

Imagine that you have a bad cold. You're sitting around drinking orange juice, watching television, and feeling pretty "blah." You'd rather be outside riding your bike.

Suddenly, you feel like sneezing. You reach for a facial tissue, but it's too late. Ah-choo! You sneeze. Thousands of tiny drops of mucus come exploding from your nose and mouth. You can't see most of them. They fly through the air at speeds of more than 100 miles per hour.

Then, after floating about in the air for a few minutes, they sink to the ground. Some land as far away as twelve feet.

Just after you sneeze, your brother comes into the room to watch television with you. He goes to the TV and tries to change the channel. He even picks up your glass and tries to drink some of your orange juice. You finally tell him to get lost, and he leaves.

WAIT FOR ME !!!

BOMBS AWAY !

Three days later, your brother comes down with a cold. He caught it from you during those few minutes he tried to watch television with you.

There are two ways he could have caught the cold? Can you figure out what they are?

SOLUTION #1: *He could have caught the cold from breathing in the invisible drops of mucus that were in the room after you sneezed. That mucus was full of your cold virus.*

SOLUTION #2: *He could have caught the cold from touching the television set or your orange juice glass and then rubbing his eyes or nose later with his hands. The TV and glass were also covered with invisible drops of mucus.*

He probably did **not** catch the cold because he drank from your glass. Cold viruses like to get into a body through the nose or eyes – not through the mouth.

MUCUS POWER!

ONE OF YA' MUCUS—GET THE BROTHER!

ARGHH!

HOW TO KEEP FROM GETTING A COLD

1. Live by yourself in outer space.

2. Live by yourself in an underground cave.

or

3. When you are around someone who has a cold, keep your hands away from your nose and mouth. And wash your hands often.

How to Keep from Spreading a Cold

1. Move into an old bomb shelter and don't let anybody in until your cold is over.

2. Go by yourself to the bottom of the ocean in a submarine and don't come up until your cold is over.

or

3. Always use facial tissues to blow your nose, to sneeze, and to cough. And wash your hands often with your own soap and towels.

HOW TO TAKE CARE OF A COLD

What do you do to "cure" a cold? Do you sniff pepper or cinnamon? Or wash the inside of your nose with cod-liver oil? Or wear and onion around your neck? Or eat garlic and vinegar pickles?

These are a few of the things kids used to be told to do to "cure" their colds. None of these cures worked, however. The truth is, there is no cure for the common cold. A lot of scientists are trying to find a cure, but so far it remains one of the big mysteries of modern medicine.

When you get invaded by a cold, all you can really do is wait for your white blood cells to stop the invasion. Usually, that takes two or three days.

In the meantime, there are a few things you can do to make yourself feel better:

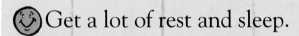 Get a lot of rest and sleep.

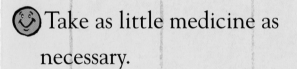 Take as little medicine as necessary.

Drink lots of healthy liquids, like fruit juices and water. They help loosen mucus and soothe a sore throat.

Blow your nose; don't sniff. Sniffing can sometimes cause ear infections.

Above all, take care of yourself. Remember, a cold is nothing to sneeze at.